You might want to
Book (Special occasion gift, to a relative or special friend, as a poem or two brings back a certain memory we share or would like to share now).

	Page	Title
1.		
2.		
3.		
4.		
5.		
6.		
	*Sample Pg. 58	Shared Paths

Your feelings or comments:

***Sample - Hi Mary, the above poems cause me to reminisce on those special times we shared - Thanks again!**

This book is dedicated to my beautiful children:
Barbara J., Douglas S., Wendy A.,
Benjamin F., and Lucas E. Weesen

Also dedicated to these special friends and colleagues in skiing:

Suzy Chaffee: Worlds Champion Free style skier,Honored member of the NSHF, multi-talented professional and poetry friend.

Nome Obermeyer: Ski business professional, and poetry friend.

Ralph 'Doc' Des Roches: Past president SIA (Ski Industry of America), Honored member of the NSHF, board member FIS (Federation International de ski). Skiing magazine; man of the Year; and my skiing and fishing friend.

Burton Boyum: Very successful Chairman NSHF. Honored member NSHF, author, colleague, and special friend'.

Poems and Pearls to ponder

First published March 2001, by Author; C. Bud Weesen

Some proceeds of each book sold will go to the National Ski Hall of Fame (NSHF) for operating costs, per agreement.

Book available from author and NSHF at address below.
Retail price $12.95 plus $2.00 S&H.
Quantity discount for 5 or more copies 'ordered from author only'

ISBN 0-9709962-0-9

C. Bud Weesen. 818 Meadowbrook Drive, West Bend, WI 53090
Phone (262) 334-2174   Fax 262-334-5890

NSHF: www.skihall E-mail: skihall@uplogon.com

*Merit Award ISP (International Society of Poets) www.poetry.com

Printed in United States by Kruepke Printing
Fax 262-334-5890

Poems and Pearls to Ponder - Available at your local book store.

FORWARD

Bud Weesen is truly a man of many talents and interests. In the 25 years I've known him, Bud has successfully accomplished whatever he has set out to do, from serving as Vice Chairman of the National Ski Hall of Fame and rubbing elbows with such skiing elite as Bill Johnson and Suzy Chaffee to skillfully building a lovely hunting lodge in the woods of Michigan where he not only hunts and fishes, but also shares his wonderful culinary skills with fellow sportsmen and friends. That this renaissance man's work has been selected for inclusion in Poetry's Elite: The Best Poets of 2000 and is now compiled in this entertaining and insightful book should, therefore, come as no surprise to anyone who knows him.

It should also come as no surprise to his friends, who are well aware of Bud's generosity, that he is donating a portion of the sales from each of his books to the National Ski Hall of Fame.

Many of us have been lucky enough to be the recipients of his poems over the years and treasure the insight, humor and inspiration in his poetry. Now others will be able to enjoy these gems that reflect Bud's keen wit, unique sense of wonder and deep spiritual faith.

So curl up in your favorite chair and enjoy, as we have, these "Poems and Pearls". Now you're among the lucky ones.

Katie Trimble Kaufman
Fortunate friend

Nationally published poems:

Page 59 1980 'Sierra Sun' - **Ski Sports Magazine**

Page 5 1995 'A Natural High' - **Treasured Poems of America**

Page 32 2000 'His Daily Love' - **ISP poetry.com**

Page 79 2000 'Touch Me' - **America at the Millennium**

Page 22 2001 'Chainsaw Man' - **Poetrys Elite - Best Poets of 2000**
(In top 33 poems chosen by: International Library of Poetry)
'The Sound of Poetry' on CD & tapes from: Poetry.com

A Natural High

A sprint on the beach an romp in the sand,
starts my heart racing as you squeeze my hand,
and the wind in our hair and warm sun on our skin,
Oh! What a high, my head fairly spins.

The patter of rain on the cabin roof,
and cozy open fire inside is really the proof,
that no one has to tell me why,
I become entranced with this natural high.

The mountain powder on a crisp cold day,
as we carv our turns and weave our way,
to the scenic valley far below,
is a winter high in the pristine snow.

The maple's fire colors and the aspen's pale yellow,
is nature's fall way to turn one mellow.
Made spectacular by the autumnal haze,
is a special high on crisp fall days.

Why, oh why, do some constantly try,
the harmful things to attain a high,
when there is so much and it's all free,
evolving daily for you and me?

"Always" and "Forever"

Words like "always" and "forever" are soothing indeed,
when used with warmth, tenderness, and love.
Like the comfort and peace, when we lift up our eyes,
and feel the presence of that someone above.

I'll never forget the look in your eyes,
and warm feelings as you said to me,
" I just can't wait my dear friend,
for that first day of "forever,"
when together we'll "always" be."

When you leave me a note, or send me a card.
I know that your feelings are really true,
'cause you sign at the end, the words I like best,
"dearest friend I'll 'always' love you."

Our Rose

'The rose' is our song,
and it reminds me of you,
the freshness of the blossom,
is our dreams coming true.

The sun and the flowers,
herald our love,
yes, it can be forever,
with His help from above

At Days End

As twilight dims and thought runs deep,
the wind has hushed, the birds asleep,
I'm lost in thought while deep inside,
a haunting feeling seems to hide.

To challenge me to reconcile the day's events,
and what lies ahead, but not circumvent,
because I must unravel the many thoughts,
and weave the pattern which means a lot.

This helps shape my tomorrow and where I'll be,
and what the future may hold for me.

It's that time of day when ones alone,
in God's embrace, His feelings shown,
and reflect on what I did today,
so the haunting feeling will fade away.

Alone

You may not agree, or just never thought,
what being alone can do,
but it's therapy we all must have,
and practiced by oh so few.

Now and then a day alone,
maybe all that you will need,
but better yet is two or more,
and after trying you will agree.

The time you choose and place to go,
are best decided just by you,
but when things are really piling up,
don't wait to make your move.

When the times at hand and you can afford,
to pick the place that is the best,
try the seashore, or mountain cabin,
for solitude, thought, and rest.

Any season is fine, but Springs the best,
when the plants start peeking through,
bathed by warm spring rains and melted snow,
they are being born anew.

Alone II

Now you're alone, breathe deep the air,
and erase the cobwebs from your mind,
let thoughts drift by like summer clouds,
and forget about the time.

You're like the Osprey soaring overhead,
carving lazy circles in the sky.
You're now relaxed and the feelings great,
the troubled world just passed you by.

Now with priorities all sorted out,
and your perspective well defined,
it's back into the 'race', but you will cope,
because alone you spent some time.

A New Year My Friend

Another year slipped by today,
so tomorrow starts anew,
and dear friend my blessings overflow,
'cause I've shared the past year with you.

The hugs we shared, the tears, and laughs,
but mostly you were always there,
to listen, and offer warmth and love,
He, and I know how much you cared.

The years have been so good to me,
but knowing you has been the best.
Last year we lost someone we loved,
and our special friendship stood the test.

The new year that's now upon us,
can be enhanced by all we share,
and each day can be so much richer,
as we touch, and love, and care.

I promised to love you always,
and you pledged the same to me.
We have a special place in each others heart,
and with God's help that will always be.

A Special Time

October sun and soft warm breeze,
that sets adrift the autumn leaves,
which flutter down to forest floor,
an exciting time to once more explore,
the woodland raptures, the trees ablaze,
with flaming colors and autumnal haze.

Normally my heart is full, an spirits high,
but today I notice a passioned sigh,
where are you my precious one,
not holding hands like we have done,
many times like this before,
please promise me there will be more.

Sights, smells, and sounds euphoric blend,
as I slowly down the trail wend.
I squeeze your hand and draw you close,
and gently kiss the lips I love the most.
I must pretend and share with you,
'cause you're the greatest love I ever knew.

Advice to Deerslayer

Deerslayer, there's three things that you should know,
if you stalk the elusive buck in the November snow.
This year I've downed my 30th buck,
and I can't agree that it's just plain luck.

These sage words of advice, you may already know,
but do you practice them when you're on the go?
What works for me, and it can for you,
is SLOW, QUIET, and a CONSTANT view.

There's also other tips to bear in mind,
if you successfully utilize your time.
Up-wind always you must go,
but rule number one is very SLOW.

His nose is keen and his ears are too,
so number two says, QUIETLY, you must move.
Alert you must stay with a CONSTANT view,
for in just two seconds he will sneak by you.

Now you've heard my tips, and if you agree,
they'll work for you, as they have for me.

A Cold Trail

The trail is long, the snow is deep,
I keep on lifting heavy feet, to seek and seek,
and push tired bones, why am I so far from home?

I started out in early morn,
refreshed and strong, a new man born.
The day grows long, the wind is sharp,
as it whips the snow around,
but push I will to seek my goal,
as I know it can be found.

Ice on my mustache is building now,
cheeks tinge as cold bites in,
but push I will, and trudge through swamps,
where large cedars fence them in.

The fingers numb inside my mitts,
yet sweat builds upon my back,
but I'll search, and search, and stumble on,
as the falling snow fills in my tracks.

A Search for Words

I search for words, my dearest friend,
but they are so elusive, when I try,
'cause I want to explain just how you make me feel,
but are you real, or just a dream in yonder sky?

That smile, the laugh, are always there,
your depth of beauty, your sense of care,
the eyes so warm, and gentle touching hands,
why you have this all I can't understand.

But best of all you share with me,
the touch, the laugh, a heart so free,
and it must be big 'cause it's so full of love,
a special purpose in design by Him above.

All this, and more, I just can't describe,
the words elude me, but I have tried.
May I humbly request a promise my dear,
to continue to share your love, for many more years.

Beach Walker

What's on your mind,
as you sift the sand,
between your toes,
in this bare foot land.

Is it the ceaseless,
pounding of the sea,
or the resulting changes,
you're so eager to see?

Driftwood is bleached and etched,
within its path,
and so artistically tumbled and shaped,
by this timeless bath.

Or might it be the seaside air,
cleansed like the sand,
and so abundant there,
for those like you who really care?

Or might it be the treasures found,
on every beach these do abound,
a stone, a shell, or driftwood art,
in each nature's hand has played a part?

Do you often tread this surf side sand,
intrigued by His the master's hand?
How nice to discover and enjoy with you,
this seaside world experienced by so few.

Beach Days

The sound of the waves on this gorgeous day,
has a soothing effect that is beyond compare.
A warm stirring breeze in the tree tops play,
and how refreshing is the lakeside air.

The gentle roll of the waves with frothy tops,
spills clean water way up on the sand.
I hope this rhythmic motion today won't stop,
as it's an experience few understand.

This splashing surf and the gentle breeze,
are complimented by a cloudless sky,
and as these waves tumble and tease,
the seagulls gracefully soar on high.

The sun on bare skin penetrates deep,
as only and open fire and sun can do.
And days like this I'll relish and keep,
but I would like to share them with you.

The waves tumble and splash as they cleanse the sand,
and join the elements combined on this day,
like smells and sounds and sights so grand,
all free to enjoy, as we travel on our way.

Back to Normal

"Back to normal," what do you mean?
Is this a dream, 'cause as you bump along the road
of life, be set with hazards and torn with strife,
what is normal, pure fantasy?

Now be realistic and face the fact,
what's yesterday's normal may not ever come back.
When briefly things are going right,
relax, enjoy, but don't lose sight.
Or be naive, and settle in,
'cause changes come like shifting winds.

Each ones "normal" can't be defined,
or programmed in your computer to recall in time.
If you have the answer friend tell me how,
'cause what's happening today is only normal for now.

Bens 8th Grade Graduation

Like a Yo Yo, or a basketball,
You have had your ups and downs,
Sometimes a very studious student,
but too often like a clown.

For eight years now you plodded on,
like a ship without a rudder,
and we hoped your reckless attitude,
would not effect Luke, your little brother.

We all knew you have it in you,
to finish right on top,
but after several real good surges,
your 'Lamborghini' sputtered to a stop.

Now here you are graduating,
with a diploma in your hand,
we are all so very proud of you,
and 'Laser Kitty' thinks it's grand.

Remember how often I told you,
but " Only" when things were going great,
"like father like son,"
a proud young man you too will make!!!

Well, anyway, you made it,
and we're proud of how well you've done.
Your Mothers very special boy,
but Fathers extra special son.

Chicago

How far away my small town seems,
at sunrise on this day,
Chicago's Loop is close at hand,
as O'hare guides in the planes.

I'm real small town,
it's not just a dream,
'cause I've hiked the forest paths,
and pulled many trout from the streams.

But you Chicago, on this day,
come through to me in a different way.

I've visited here many times before,
but, like all big cities, I did deplore,
your wall to wall traffic, and big jets roar,
as they seek the skies which they explore.

This morning your tall buildings, in mist inshrined,
seem to reach up to all mankind,
and beckon with a warmth, to share with them,
the exciting treasures that lie within.

You can just sense, the air travelers stare,
as they look in awe as they near O'hare.
Unbelievable - and it will always be,
all the planes afloat, on this airway sea.

Chicago, you've got so many sights,
and they're fun to share with you,
and I'm sure glad this small town guy,
has looked you over with a different view.

Christmas Morn '81

At 5:30am on the day of Christ's birth,
my wife arose to get ready for church.
Her footsteps on stairway a light pitter-patter,
as she checked out our furnace to see what's the matter.

I snuggled deeply down in my soft warm bed,
as visions of sugar cookies were adrift in my head.
An unusual furnace smell entered her nose,
as the smoke from our fireplace up the chimney it rose.

I in my pajamas and she now in her sweater,
I could tell by her voice the smell was no better.
She finally got in her car and turned on the lights,
and I mumbled merry xmas from bed,
as she drove out of sight.

Conscience

You should have one, but is it there,
when you do something wrong do you really care?
You can feel it way down deep inside,
and you will feel uneasy, but where to hide.

Are you often quick to judge someone else,
when you've done something similar your own self?
Have you denied the charge and wouldn't budge,
remember He said, "don't judge lest ye be judged?"

You should really heed His advice, and His alone,
"You that have not sinned cast the first stone."
Can you deny the charge, and have never erred,
or are there "two rules" and you don't really care?

I hope my friend that your conscience is clear,
and you're ready for judgement when His voice you hear.
Now, you should feel your conscience when He calls,
as He is the "final" one, to judge us all.

You can clear your conscience, and have the chance,
don't you think it's time, your life to enhance?
It was on Calvary's Cross for all to see,
He gave us the chance for our conscience to free.

Oh, what a feeling, when you purged yourself,
as it's much more important than "anything" else.
My friend I know, 'cause I've taken the test,
so now into Eternity my soul will rest. Amen

Chainsaw Man

Every hunting camp should have a chainsaw man,
and if you heard him snore you'd understand.
He started with us some forty years ago,
and was a good deer tracker in the fresh snow.

Chainsaw lost his teeth a few years ago,
and he now shuffles from bed to table a wee bit slow.
The corn cob pipe held firmly in his gums,
and he puffs blue smoke 'till we're overcome.

His last pipe finished he shuffles to bed,
and now comes the time his huntin' pals dread.
This chain saw starts with a little snore,
but brace yourself for a whole lot more.

At times that saw will really purr,
and you'd swear he's knotchin' a douglas fir,
Then it burbles and barks like it's low on gas,
and you pray to God the noise won't last.

Now the saw is quiet so let's try to sleep,
we sure don't get much during the huntin' week.
It sure is noisy, but here's our plan,
we're installing a new muffler on the chainsaw man.

Daily Hugs

How much better is each passing day,
with a nice warm hug and friendly touch,
as we pass along our way, while we are involved,
in work or play.

Remember friend to take the time,
and share some love with me,
as even one daily hug will do the job,
for it's the most effective therapy.

The warmth that flows from me to you,
when the hug is genuine,
is very difficult to explain,
but it happens each, and every time.

Count your blessings each passing day,
while you hug a friend along the way.
The feelings great and you'll agree,
so practice it my friend then you will see.

To The Bakery "Boys"

Bob and Rich's, "Old Fashioned Bakery," is kind a' like home,
and after over six years affiliation, I must write a poem!!
I visit there often, a warm (ovens!), friendly place,
but don't get in their way, 'cause it's always a 'race!!!

Bobs shouting, out orders, with his hands in the dough,
while Rich, and 'Sgt. Debbie', monitor cash flow.
Stocking the ovens daily, we call him 'Rev.' Sid,
and 'cranking' out tasty bakery, is 'Billy the kid'!!!

Patty and Sue 'push' tasty treats in the store,
and 'some times' the customers, return for some more!!
Bob lets you know, he never makes a mistake,
but check the spelling close, as he letters the cake!!!

Rich,Kevin, & Tom, sometimes look busy, and also 'fryer' Dan,
Gerry keeps the place 'sparkling,' and John's a 'talkative', man.
I just drink my coffee, laugh, and keep up the teasin',
and hope all of the crew has a happy holiday season.

Dreamin'?

Just a dream you say, or fantasy,
I'll not agree.
Not long ago I saw you there,
the bluest eyes and hair so fair,
a breath of spring, your lingering smile,
I'll not forget, tho' its been a while.

Soft spoken words revealed the charm,
and deep within a treasure lays,
to share with me another day.

You touched my life, its not been the same,
I've searched, and searched, not all in vain,
'cause I know your close,
as you extend your hand,
to fulfill our dreams, and long time plans.

Enjoy Every Day

As you awake, each and every day,
the world is at your door,
but it's all up to you and how you plan,
to utilize the treasures that are in store.

Don't just rely on others help,
but use what the Lord gave you,
as we all have countless abilities,
but we utilize so few.

To make the most of what you have,
work daily at staying fit,
as physical and mental attitudes,
deteriorate rapidly when you quit.

Take heed of the many handicapped,
and how they live that way,
and count the blessings that you have,
and you'll enjoy each passing day.

Forgiving

Please forgive them Father,
for they know not what they do,
spoke the voice from the cross, for both me and you.
With shoulders heavily burdened,
with all the worldly sins,
He asked us to unload them, and bring them all to Him.

Yes, He died to make us Holy,
to be faithful, and be free,
to prove His Father's love, for all the world to see.
We must try to understand His lessons,
taught daily in His life, like forgiveness, and compassion,
to our fellow man, and others in our life.

Are we so very perfect,
not ever once to err,
and criticize each other, like we do not seem to care?
We must forgive, and listen carefully,
to the one's hurt that's really felt,
as He forgives us freely, when on our knees we've knelt.

The virtues of compassion and understanding,
can be rewarding in many ways,
as we reach out in forgiving, each and every day.
I've promised to be forgiving,
as I try to understand your plight,
will you do the same for me, as it will help to make it right?

Friend Chick-a-dee

Little chick-a-dee, you're sure a light hearted friend,
regardless of weather and season.
How fortunate are we who will take the time,
to watch your antics, and constant play teasin'.

You're always fluffing your feathers,
and hanging upside down.
You're constantly fluttering about,
you tiny black - capped clown.

Your chick-a-dee song is sure apropos,
and you continually chatter whether sunshine or snow.

He must have been happy,
when He first "wound your spring,"
and watched you flutter about,
and heard the song that you sing.

You bring a smile to the shut-in,
as they watch your window side play,
but how lucky are we,
who can see, and hear you each day.

Hand in Hand

Friend, will you walk with me, hand in hand,
and enjoy what's free, in this beautiful land.
We'll smell the flowers, and hear the many songs,
of the birds that sing in this world they belong.

The wind in the pines, and how good they smell,
their stories would be interesting, if only they'd tell.
The sun is so warm, as we gaze up high,
and watch the fluffy white clouds, in the endless blue sky.

The gentle lap of the surf, as it cleanses the sand,
it's here we'll go barefoot, hand in hand.
He created these things, so beautiful and free,
will you accept my offer, to enjoy them with me?

Friend thank you for walking with me, hand in hand,
to enjoy what's free, in this beautiful land.
You're squeezing my hand now, is it to say,
"thank you friend, I've had a wonderful day."

Happiness

What is so common to young and old,
and rich and poor alike,
as they explore the complex avenues,
on the trip throughout their life?

That goal on distant horizon,
and most always out of reach.
The methods used are often devious,
as the answers we must seek.

Of course you know it's happiness,
pursued first by early man,
and as centuries slipped swiftly by,
you'd think we would have developed a perfect plan.

O yeah, then why do we often repeat,
like a rekindling of a flame,
the very things that destroy this goal,
like greed, wealth, and worldly fame.

No one seems to have the answers,
but conscientiously they try,
and you can see it in the deeds they do,
also in their vitality, and love of life,
as the years slip swiftly by.

The most important ingredient is love,
but first you have to love yourself,
then you'll find that it's fun to share,
and it's now that true happiness is felt.

He's Always There

The blessings so rich from the One above,
can I ever repay your constant love?
Your with me daily where ever I go,
I am constantly aware of it, but this you know.

The day I knelt and called to you,
to direct my life and to start anew,
you listened then and reached for my hand,
why oh why, I can't understand.

Was it because I was so sincere,
and needed so badly for you to hear,
my plaitive call and promises made,
and my total heart to you I gave?

Yes, you were right there and daily are,
and never more than a prayer a far,
as you see the results of promises made,
I'll honor them all 'cause my promise I gave.

His Daily Love

How blessed is the One above,
who gave me the chance to live and love,
all things created by His hand,
and woven so beautifully in the master plan.

I must thank Him daily for what He's done,
before or after, the setting sun,
and live the life that He intends,
unto my fellow man my love must blend.

How rich and full our life can be,
remember Him daily and you'll agree,
that He asks so little, but is always there,
with open arms 'cause He really cares.

It Isn't Fair

That word 'Love' so often used,
but why so vainly it we choose,
to express ones self and how we feel,
but are we real,
or like a facade we're not sincere,
when it may hurt some one so dear.

It isn't fair if we can't accept,
the one we hold special with no regrets,
and take them just the way they are,
no matter if we don't approve,
of things they choose, and what they do,
or want to be, and return our love,
but yet be free.

If you say," I love you," and do imply,
they are someone very special, and you will try,
to understand just what they are,
and who they really want to be, just like you,
and yes, like me.

At times we just can't understand,
why things don't go as we have planned,
and why they did what we can't approve,
but remember they must choose, or we will lose,
the one we say we really love, and this means care,
so hold them close, or it isn't fair.

Keep Truck'n

Hey you! why are you always in high gear?
Keep pushing - you may not be around next year.
How do you ever sustain such drive?
No way you can get out of this world alive.

Must be exciting to watch your estate grow,
what's wrong with those who move slow?
We know you'd help the needy if you had time,
and bought the blind man's pencil if you had a dime.

Who says that you never get to church,
last Christmas & Easter in a back pew you perched.
Some year you'll write your Mom & Dad,
when they pass on will you really be sad?

Just remember we are proud of you,
so stay in high gear and on the move.
When you leave this world it'll be a sad day,
but we'll divide your estate and start to play.

Believe me friend you have my respect,
as I drive my Caddy to get my welfare check,
Also I must remember to get my food stamps,
and trade them for a bottle and head for camp!!

Knight Time

Like Knights of old we sally forth,
to slay our daily dragon,
but why, oh why, as twilight comes,
it's our tail that's really draggin'.

When dawn breaks new and we're all refreshed,
the exciting worlds right at our door,
so pull on your armor and mount your horse,
and venture out into the world to score.

The valor earned will be bestowed,
and it's just what you will need,
as you gallantly sit upon the saddle,
of your tired returning steed.

Your princess waits at castle door,
in gold gilded gown and long hair in curls,
while over the rampart your 'coat of arms',
on pennant flag the wind unfurls.

Now I yawn, stretch, and rub tired eyes,
as I peek out the window shade,
for it's a rainy day, so back to bed,
a lousy knight I'd probably made.

Mantle of White

The breeze overhead is gentle now,
as it stirs the sentinel pines.
A foot of new snow lies on the ground,
and we've slipped into the Winter time.

Today the woods are born anew,
with this mantle of snowy white.
The bears asleep, and the chippy too,
and we've seen the last goose flight.

How fortunate am I to live this day,
and experience what's all around,
the pristine creeks, and forest too,
where wildlife does abound.

The sun's rays probe the crisp cold air,
and beautifies this day.
The snow caps sparkle on the stumps,
touched by a fairy's wand I'd say.

The nuthatch searches the hemlock bark,
for the insects hidden there,
while close by his friends, the chick a dees,
flutter playfully through the air.

The crossbill opens the hemlock cones,
as only they can do,
and the pine siskin is a busy one,
and he's not afraid of you.

Mantle of White: page II

To pause and watch our feathered friends,
and breathe deep the clean cold air,
just pleasant thoughts flow through my mind,
and I'm sure glad I'm here.

The balsam's boughs bend down with snow,
as I weave my way through them,
and they too sparkle in the sun,
like piles of brilliant gems.

Don't ever pass a balsam's bough,
without running it through your hand,
as it's a scent we try to duplicate,
which is easy to understand.

A day like this is rare indeed,
and I'd share it friend with you,
and you too should really take the time,
as He made it for you too.

Miracle of Birth

How does the tiny little seed become a giant Oak,
and what happens when Spring rains a garden do soak?
With the help of God's sun, as it shines forth each day,
lifts crocus, daffodils, and tulips to a brilliant color display.

The fragrance of lilacs on the soft spring breeze,
the sudden cloak of green from shiny new leaves,
and the flap of colored wings as butterflies rise from cocoons,
where they have slept all winter in Egyptian like tombs.

These wonders of Nature emerge every day,
like the wobbly spotted fawns in a May field at play.
Cute fuzzy little kitty as it paws the ball of yarn,
soon to play a bit more serious with a mouse in the barn.

The clumsy furry puppy with a cool wet nose,
we see you hiding, an ready to pounce, from under the pile of clothes.
Each birth is so exciting, as He planned it that way,
like the miracle of the sperm, on a most special day.

Deep inside the fertile egg so eagerly waits,
the arrival of the sperm, by its designated mate.
The first positive signs in four to six weeks,
signal the success of sperm and egg in the goal they seek.

Now the excitement will build as her body discovers,
the change within and felt only by Mothers.
Soon the father can see that her tummy is growing,
and you can tell he's so proud by his eyes always glowing.

Now the sound of the new heart, and movement within,
can be heard by them both, and felt also by him.
Dear wife, you're such a cute "little tease,
the twinkle in your eyes says," Lucas or Ashley Louise?"

My Three Strengths

As one matures and thoughts run deep,
our values change in what we seek.
Now when we pause, search, and reflect,
our values should merit much more respect.

My top priority is "Strength" alone,
to make my body a more perfect home.
It must house my priorities three,
or that happy person I will never be.

My "Spiritual Strength" is right on top,
and I must practice it daily and never stop.
My "mental strength" runs a close second,
it too must be exercised daily, as twilight years beckon.

My "physical strength" is number three,
and I must stay as strong as I can be.
How easy to be complacent, but I'm not naive,
for it's me, and me alone, that I will deceive.

My Outlook

My friend, how fortunate you really are,
if you enjoy like me,
each and every passing day,
whether there's sun, or rain, or sleet.

Do you, as I, when you arise each morn,
look forward to each day?
Breathe deep the air and smile a smile,
whether it's off to work or play?

No matter if it's raining still,
as it has for most a week.
The earthly plants can drink their fill,
and how clean are walks and streets.

Oh! Sunrise, you're so great today,
it's like being born anew.
So many take you just for granted,
and they won't pause, to enjoy the view.

Wow! how the snow swirls all about,
as it blows throughout the night.
I can hardly wait for tomorrow's dawn,
to enjoy the artistic sights.

My Outlook II

How can you ignore these beautiful dawns,
and grumble when you awake.
It sure won't help to make your day,
so smile for heavens sake!

Are you so busy most every day,
like many seem to be,
that you can't pause to drink you fill,
of what's so beautiful and free?

Why dont you try with tomorrow's dawn,
regardless of the day,
to first put on your most pleasant smile,
'cause it's lots more fun that way.

Those that meet you will be surprised,
and they will become infected too,
'cause what's so beautiful down deep inside,
will flow from me and you.

My Friend Marie

Marie, dear friend, you're Oh so special,
and how fortunate for me,
to have been allowed ten years ago,
to have met someone like thee.

We all scurry through this busy world,
and make a lot of friends,
but ones like you are far between,
and I hope our friendship never ends.

Your beauty radiates from deep inside,
and in looks you got your share,
How very lucky for one like me,
where your touch shows how much you care.

Your dress is 'always' tastefully done,
enhanced by a figure, oh so trim.
A lovely smile, and sparkle in your eyes,
reflects the beauty from deep within.

How unfortunate for one like me,
who sees you only now and then,
but I promise to cherish every one,
will you do the same my dear, dear friend?

"My Reflections"

How many times through out your life,
do you pause to recollect,
of the times gone by, today, and tomorrow,
where there is so much to reflect.

These reflections give us food for thought,
as we formulate life's plan.
Are we best to go it all alone,
or try to mesh with our fellow man?

Listen friends to what hearts say,
'cause they most often do reflect,
those important feelings learned from life,
and to be used on our future treck.

This morning at dawn I need this time,
as I walk along the tranquil lake.
I must reflect on past and present,
to determine if a new direction I must take.

How very fortunate I have been,
as my reflections I review,
and the many blessing that He's shared,
most experienced by oh so few.

The twilight years too soon arrive,
when all we do is sit and reflect,
so friend do as I and plan your time,
a fuller life will await you, and much more than you expect.

Nightfall

The wind has hushed,
the birds are still,
as night settles all about.

The mirrored surface of the pond,
emits the splash of feeding trout.

How quiet,
and oh, so tranquil,
gone are the sounds of day.

Now all the nocturnal creatures,
romp through the woods at play.

Author

No Waist!

What's happened to that tiny waist,
I used to hold, as I gave chase,
along the beach in summer fun,
while we laughed, and frolicked in the sun.

That black bikini, oh, so trim,
made more for looks than used to swim.
Those two red words were meant to tease,
what did they say? Pray tell me please.

You were petite, in every way,
a sharp neat dresser I would say.
In fashion jeans you were so cute,
I'm glad we bought you cowboy boots.

The figure trim - a rare work of art,
but way out of proportion was your heart.
It was so very big down deep inside,
but as it overflowed it couldn't hide.

We loved, and laughed, those precious times,
Oh, how you've aged like vintage wine.
Every month now your waist expands,
the tiny life inside does make demands.

Honey, I still can see that tiny waist,
I'd like to explain though - just in case,
you really do know that I love the change,
after all it's me who's 'half' the blame!!

Northwoods Reverie

Alone today I trek these woods,
as I've done countless times before,
but I've never felt solitude so serene,
and I'm overwhelmed, though I know what's in store.

Friend, try as I will, I just can't explain,
but how fulfilling if I could share this with you.
You just have to be here on, Oh, such a day,
as I know you would feel like I do.

I'm miles in the woods at my small rustic cabin,
with a whole week ahead to explore,
and I'll be on the trail from dawn to dusk,
as I have countless times before.

It's November month with four inches of snow,
and now noon on this most precious day.
The sun high in the sky and is really warm,
and a teasin' wind floats nice smells by my way.

Inhale deeply of balsam and sun drenched pine,
it's a mixture only nature can blend.
It's on a day like this that you can see forever,
and how much fuller will be my life when it ends.

Northwoods Reverie: page II

The smells and the sights on this glorious day,
makes me so humble, 'cause I just can't explain.
The other ingredient is the variety of sounds,
and it's a blend not even a conductor could arrange.

The bubbling, and gurgle, of a trailside spring,
like youthful laughter as it flows on its way.
The red squirrel's chatter tells of his new winter coat,
and what's on the mind of the sassy blue jay?

The staccato sounds of a downey woodpecker,
as he taps away on a hollow old tree,
and the wee chickadee calls as they flutter about,
and feed up side down in the trees around me.

Now that teasin' wind as it searches about,
playfully bounces the evergreen's bough.
Just remember my friend this won't last forever,
so do like me and participate now.

Today's sundrenched forest with its mantle of snow,
and the sounds, and sights, with the smells blended in.
If given the chance you must take the time,
'cause to not is really a sin.

Where Ya Going

How the twigs bent so grows the tree,
that's sage advice so please take heed.
Step back today and check your sights,
as they are aimed so goes your life.

Author

Old Cedar Tree

Oh, large leaning cedar tree,
with boughs outstreched,
you're so very welcome today.
This November rain and sleet,
is so cold and wet,
as I hike along my way.

Now as I rest my back,
against your wide trunk,
while your boughs hold off the rain.
My rifle leans against your dry bark,
and how majestically over the forest you reign.

Priorities

A lifetime competing from birth until death,
is cause for remorse less our mind we refresh,
as we scurry along the corridor of life,
so often riddled with failure, disappointment and strife.

How lucky are those, who early in years,
stores in his mind some advice from his peers,
but not all that he hears!!
For that active young mind is sorting things out,
as he knows what he wants, and what's life really about.

The ambiance he enjoys resoundingly rings,
how fragrant the flowers, and how varied the songs,
that his feathered friends sing,
as they wing thru the air, excited by freedom,
and no earthly cares.

Look about you my friend at those loaded with wealth,
where the most precious commodity is ones own good health.
If you can't enjoy the competition, as an every day game,
utilize life's natural ingredients to remain happily fulfilled,
and hopefully stay sane!!

If you don't enjoy competing in life's vicious every day games,
refrain from a life of castle building,
as it's truly insane.

Raven Talk

This northern forest is quiet today,
except for the ravens, who forage and play.
The still air is pierced by their raucous cry,
while their flapping wings stir the leaden sky.
A slight snow cover clings to the ground,
as tiny snow flakes sift softly down.

I've listened to the ravens for many years,
and understand well each call I hear.
Three "wak,wak,waks," lets the world know,
something approaches their meal on the snow.
The big motley old birds have a deep throaty call,
it's one long "waak," that explains it all.

The younger birds while developing their call,
give two short high "auk,auks," their first summer and Fall.
When they are being sassy, and silly at play,
they give three to five "auks" while they cruise on their way.

The other call that's most often heard,
is a deep "auk,auk," from a contented bird.
This lets all know that he's well fed,
but he's still on the search for something dead.
Listen my friend, as I always do,
and find out what the ravens are telling you.

Real Love?

What do we have if there's no Love,
especially one blessed by Him above?
Deep down in your heart is someone there,
who shares your love, and truly cares?

I had this before, and oh how great,
she valued my love, and did reciprocate.
Our hearts entwined, so full of peace,
such exciting days, as joys we'd seek.

This special friend so enhanced my life,
we tied the knot, became man and wife.
I worshiped her and she seemed to care,
as we went hand in hand most everywhere.

My darling, our vows, "to never part,"
I thought were etched on "both" our hearts.
We laughed and played for several years,
held each other close, and knew no fear.

A problem was there before we wed,
but we would get through, we agreed and said,
'cause with our love, the very best,
would certainly survive and stand the test.

Is love really blind, as the saying goes,
and is it only the Lord who really knows?
You often promised to be right there,
'cause you were sincere and really cared.

Now to all my friends, I caution you,
is yours really love, and is it true?
Our temporary excitement, which seemed so right,
as we snuggled so close each and every night.

Oh my dear, we can prove they're wrong,
and show them all, that together we belong.
The love we knew seemed the very best,
so let's unite our hearts, and once again be blessed.

"Reflections"

Wispy tendrils of vapor arise this morn',
from the woodland pond to once again be born.
In the leaden sky when as raindrops they'll fall,
bye and bye, to pok mark the pond's surface,
as they skip about,
and tease the sleek feeding native trout.

This warm clear Spring day, where these trout lay,
gentle buffs the pond's surface so cold and clear,
where Winter's ice recently disappeared,
and heralded a new season this time of year.

Nature's calendar, the reflections make,
as one watches the surface of a small forest lake,
or on the pond where colored leaves float and spin,
and where Canadian flight honkers recently dropped in.

Like puffs of cotton on a bright warm summer day,
these clouds chase the sky, while happy at play,
and laugh at themselves in the mirror below,
of the pond's surface as they skitter, to and fro.

The muskrat's mouth stuffed with tender greens,
plys the pond's surface as she swims up stream,
to feed the small bundles of fir,
nestled deep in the pond's bank, so anxious for her,

These daily nature reflections that one can read,
like a book, and how lucky for those,
who take the time to look, and for nary a price,
this book's cover is open from warm spring rains,
'till all reflections are coated with ice.

River of Life

Many of times I've pondered the thought,
how our life is like a creek.
If flows, and grows, and reaches out,
as new experiences we seek.

Our life begins a small pure spring,
not knowing where to go,
but it reaches out to find its way,
as the days increase its flow.

The obstacles that first arise,
define path, that we must take,
like rocks and logs that lay ahead,
our future they help shape.

Knowledge, and experience, like feeder streams,
increases our size and flow,
and provide the strength that we will need,
as we mature and grow.

From spring, then creek, a stream evolves,
over spilling its banks at times,
to nourish the many tender plants,
that start their eager climb.

We too must reach out to help and share,
as often as we can,
and extend our knowledge every day,
to help our fellow man.

The bubbling, dancing, youthful stream,
joins others on the way,
but now it's a river, and so serene,
and it no longer seems to play.

Now the river calms as days slip by,
and mingles with waters in the bay.
Its identity no longer shows,
in this world its had its day.

Pretend Hunter

Lo to the "hunter" who baits the deer,
and peeks from concealed blind year after year.
While the real hunter utilizes both skill and luck,
as he tracks the forest for his elusive buck,

The real hunter on foot has sights to enjoy,
while the pretend hunter wastes time in his concealed ploy.
The big buck is often shot by the hunting man,
while it was enroute to the "baited" stand!!

Sage Advice

By beaver pond I sit today,
my minds adrift and it's okay.
Against a sunny stump I rest my rear,
I'm low on gas and out of gear.

On warm sunny days you must relax,
forget the buck and his big tracks.
This therapy we all can use,
so now's the time to take a snooze.

Slow up my friend and please take heed,
a spot like this is what you need.
But if one like this can not be found,
try any other sunny soft piece of ground.

Seaside Memories

**A warm gentle breeze playfully teases the trees,
and enhances the balmy summer day here by the beach,
where soothing waves reach, and reach,
to erase bare footprints as I tread the warm sand,
Wishing I was walking with you hand in hand.**

**Humids the air with seashore smells,
Oh! how I want to share and not just tell, you my love,
now so far away, but you are right here in my heart,
on this so special day.**

**We've played and loved so often here,
as my mind drifts back to yesteryear, where I can
hear your laughter, while holding your hand,
as we frolicked and romped in this clean white sand.**

**I can still smell the sun on your skin and hair,
Oh! what fragrance, it's there, it's there.
No wonder I care, and love you so,
to constantly hold you close, never to let you go.**

**He repeats these days of scents and sounds,
here by the seashore they do abound,
to refresh our memories and enjoy again,
with the one I love, and my warm thoughts within.**

**Friend, my darling, euphoric I am,
today while walking barefoot in 'our' sand.
Your in my heart, and thoughts, in so many ways,
even though you're so very far away.**

Searching

How far away tonight you seem,
I'm reaching out, but like in a dream,
You're reaching too, but slowly drift away,
like a rudderless ship on a distant bay.

I want to run, but where to go,
your tracks erased in the light falling snow,
and the evenings hushed as I call to you,
it's all in vain, but this I knew.

My heart's beat is rapid as I quicken' my pace,
I can see you there but can't touch your face,
so please, oh please, reach for my hand,
I need you now can't you understand.

I once held you close but then let you go,
so I keep on searching in this trackless snow.
Oh! please once more do hold me tight,
so I can stop my search on this snowy night.

"SENTIMENTAL"

How rich and rare, if you can share,
those many sentimental things,
like hand holding days and all forays,
and most special, wedding rings.

The mesmerized feeling by fireplace,
and clean sunny beach with crashing waves,
going hand in hand with barefoot prints in sand,
on those fantastic summer days.

My clothes so large, I shared with you,
and they held a warm and special meaning,
and you looked just great with a happy face,
as you also did, with your 'social' evening preening.

Warm gentile smile, your natural style,
and soft warm voice when you were amorous.
I called you 'Funny Face', & meant no disgrace,
'cause to me you are so glamorous.

The nitely backrubs with "double" lotion,
you know were more than, 'just your share',
but like splitting our meals, when dining out,
were fun, and revealed our true love, and care.

These sentimental things, with a happy ring,
are fondly etched upon our hearts,
and these 'nostalgic thoughts' will often return,
and we pray God we'll never part.

Shared Paths

Let's not forget this beautiful world,
spread daily at our door,
and the many paths that we discover,
and with whom we do explore.

Shared times are very special,
the warmth we give and we receive,
so let's slow our pace a wee bit,
and touch base as we proceed.

I know, as I, you do reflect,
on moments so serene,
when we were oh so very close,
and you know just what I mean.

I think about you often,
and hope your path will wind my way,
'cause the tender times together,
pray God wont fade away.

I'll promise to do my part,
and keep you ever on my mind,
and if this is not too much to ask,
wont you try to share sometime?

Sierra Sun

Sierra Sun you're riding high,
adrift today in Tahoe's sky.
It's late in May and the lakes breeze is cool,
but your solar rays warm the mountain pools.

From a lofty site you do your thing,
From the early snows to the thaws of Spring.
this Tahoe basin where tall pines stand,
evolved so beautifully from His master plan.

The touch of frosting on this natural cake,
are your sparking reflections on this pristine lake.

My midwest home is far away,
but many times I've come here to play.
How fortunate are we, and it's open to all,
to ski and enjoy the mountains tall.

As you cast your rays over this beautiful land,
help us keep it open to every man.
We skier's, and others, want to share,
your precious warm days in the mountain air.

Please help us preserve from the selfish ones,
who want to legislate out these places in the Sun.
The hiker's and campers are relatively few,
and we'd share it with them these days under you.

Sierra Sun may I very often return,
to enjoy you with all others who share this concern.

Sleepy Little Black Bear

Little black bear you sleepy head,
don't you know it's time for bed.
We see your tracks daily where ever we go,
and it sure must be cold on bare feet in the snow.

Didn't your mom tell you to be fast asleep,
when the north wind blows in snow and sleet?
Sure it's been warm the last few days,
and the snow is melting from the suns rays.

One has to smile when we see your tracks,
you pad up the hill and slide right back.
You must be having loads of fun,
in your first snow and the bright warm sun.

We've followed your tracks the last three days,
as you snooped for a den and puttered and played.
I saw where you followed me yesterday,
and seemed so puzzled when I turned the wrong way.

Doesn't your tail get cold when you occasionally sit?
I'd sure like to see you at a time like this.
And what did you think when you sat on the bluff,
and scanned your domain you fuzzy little tough?

Sleepy little black bear with your warm thick fur,
your mom was wise so listen to her.
Find your den and crawl into sleep,
as tomorrow the snow might be two feet deep.

Smile

How do you expect me to be grumpy all day,
when you unleash that smile in so pleasant a way.
If I want to be unhappy, it's sure up to me,
but darn it's hard when you smile, and I like what I see.

The day may start overcast, all shivery and cold,
but then you turn on that smile, and low and behold,
you've screwed it all up as out comes the sun,
and we chalk up another day filled with fun.

Ok, you convinced me, and I'll try it awhile,
but my friends wont believe it when I turn on my smile.

Special Friends

Phyllis Varled, Author, April Bryant - Lander
At ISP convention - Washington D.C.

Are you really aware of what friends are for,
or do you just take them all in stride?
You must pause at times and evaluate,
'cause you'll understand when once you tried.

First reflect on all the things you've shared,
the highs, and those important lows.
Were they right there when you needed them,
and did warm feelings seem to flow?

When you are really riding high,
it seems friends are everywhere,
but we all at times really hit the skids,
now there's oh so few who care.

How easy it is to rationalize,
when you cannot spare the time,
but now place yourself in this same spot,
where those special friends are hard to find.

Throughout your life friends come and go,
but there's always those special few,
who are sincere, and want to keep in touch,
you must let them, as there love is true.

As your life unfolds you'll realize,
that your greatest wealth is friends,
so do invest more of yourself,
as it will return precious dividends.

Dear Friend

No greater pleasure can be found,
than to have a friend like you,
who loves the forests, lakes, and streams,
and most other things I do.

Dear friend I cherish our promise,
to always, and ever, share our time,
so please hold tight my hand and walk with me,
and those 'magical moments' we will find.

Suzy Chaffee, Author, Allen and Marie Adezio

Adezio's

Friends Allen and Marie,
you're two of a kind,
how lucky are we,
you're a treasure to find.

Now don't swell up with ego,
and start strutting about,
and list your success,
with one 'Giant' shout!!!

Of course you know that's my humor,
as you always have my respect,
let our friendship endure,
when we pause to reflect.

Sounds

The piter-pater of gently falling rain,
and the Northwind rattling the window pane.
Children's laughter, while enthralled in games,
the snap and crackle of hearth-side flames,
are just some of the sounds we come to know,
as through the years we so quickly grow.

The poor deaf ones who sit and stare,
what kind of sounds are really there,
that turns ones head so quickly, then smiles,
they're told it's 'humor', when all the while,
they sit in silence, can't understand,
when they ask for answers, and at times demand.

The seagulls call, while enjoying their play,
over the crashing surf on a summer day.
White Throated sparrow empties his heart,
with joyful songs by a roadside park.
The purr of a kitten, and the puppies growl,
are everyday sounds we know so well.

The twilight haunting call of a pair of loons,
the wolf's spine tingling howl, under a full moon.
A great horned owl hoots, as he searches for prey,
and the field mouse squeaks in the meadow at play.
The bubbling brook, has such a soothing sound,
and there's countless others that richly abound.

The city folk enjoy their own daily sounds,
like traffic scurrying around the town,
and the big jets cruising overhead,
and other hot summer nights sounds, as they lay in bed.
Even on deaf ones ears these sounds do fall,
but, oh, how lucky for us who can hear them all.

Spring Time Fantasy

Drip by drip it starts to grow,
from the sugar maple tree,
as the sap awakens and starts its flow,
and what an exciting spring sight to see.

Starry nights with a breathless chill,
help produce this icy treat,
but daytime skies the sun must fill,
to entice the sap to upward reach.

The harbinger of what's to come,
is heralded by this sight,
so melt a piece upon your tongue,
and enjoy this spring delight.

The gentle breeze pushes wispy clouds,
as it enjoys the playfull chase,
above the fields so freshly plowed,
'till every cloud has been erased.

Kneel down my friend and grasp some soil,
and smell, as it tumbles from your hand,
this fresh earthly scent, as the farmer toils,
arise from furrows across our land.

Now's the time to seek a sunny spot,
with your back against a tree,
now your minds at ease with pleasant thoughts,
and you're as relaxed as you can be.

Now eye lids rest as you start to drift,
soothed by the scents and sounds,
such therapy the Springs up-lift,
and it profusely does abound.

Now the drip,drip,drip, of the maples ice,
sets the stage you will agree,
and the time you take is the only price,
to enjoy Mother Nature's Spring Fantasy.

Steel Doors

The clanging doors poor souls do deplore,
will they go on for ever more,
and deafen twice a day their ears,
this startling sound they hear, and hear?

It starts down corridors so cold,
of cement blocks where echoes grow,
and grow, from steel doors slamming,
tightly shut, with welded seams not bolt and nut.

Like steel traps with jaws so cold,
the poor animal legs they hold and hold.
The sound to repeat both day and night,
from steel doors clanging, and lock so tight.

In dungeons old the sound the same,
inside were souls who suffered pain,
each time the heavy steel doors sang,
when they slammed shut, and echoes rang.

Ancient dungeons changed to jails of old,
but the slamming doors were just as bold,
when clanged and banged in early morn,
and when slammed at night the sound was scorned.

This ear jolting sound will never change,
but it must help one's priorities to arrange,
and is the count down to what one seeks,
as free men walking a quiet street.

Note: Requested by a Special Friend.

Summer Senses

The warm gentle lake breeze
brushes softly against the pines,
scattering about the blended
fragrances, which are truly summer.

Close your eyes now and indulge,
drink your fill of these soothing sounds,
and smells, and feel the warm deeply
penetrating sun on this morning beach.

The low soaring gulls call, and answer,
while the surf gently spills upon the shore,
ever cleansing the warm sand,
it's really summer and how tranquil.

Excitingly beautiful with free repeat
performances summer after summer.
Can't you smell these special smells,
hear the sounds, and really feel it? It's beckoning you.

"Suzie"

Suzie, Suzie please pray tell,
are you just another country belle?
Of you I think I could be fond.
unless you're just a cute dumb blonde.

Is that neat fetching smile you use,
really true, or just to confuse?
My Mom warned me about girls like you,
who teased and flirted, but were not true.

I suppose that you will never tell,
but then maybe it's just as well,
'cause I could never stand the hurt,
so find someone else to tease and flirt!!!

Linda, Get it in Gear!

Like cattle drives in days of old,
they had to keep them movin'
but to get the "BIG BUTT" of yours in gear,
is something I'm not provin'!!

Note: L.C. loved this as she had a "small" butt!

Sherry

**Sherry, I met you only recently,
and I would like to know you better.
You're certainly not an average chick,
'cause you've got it all together.**

**Behind those soft blue eyes I find,
and under that neat blonde hair,
a mind that's working overtime,
producing ideas that are rare.**

**How does such a tiny one,
turn out 'great' works of art,
Please keep it up you 'dynamo',
'cause you've got a super spark!!**

Smile KTK

Blessed are those, and there are oh so few,
who have some of the traits, so prevelant in you.
I've traveled the world over, seen more than my share,
I enjoy many close friends, but none can compare.

You're a very special person, much sought after by men,
but enticingly elusive, like a precious rare gem.
Your smile is so warm, and you share it with all,
such 'genuine' compassion, one can't help being enthralled.

Your hands are beautifully graceful, and are noticed everyday,
whether pushing your hair back, when at work or at play.
Your charm is contagious, 'cause it starts deep inside,
what a neat combination, with those inviting blue eyes.

Your humor is classic, and evokes many laughs,
but one has to listen closely, or it will slip right on past.
Thank you dear 'KTK, ' for coming into my life,
what a wonderful experience, in a world torn with strife!

Our last day together, will be difficult for me,
please promise to keep in touch, 'till this life we take leave.

Susan

On June 22nd in the year '56, a new voice was heard,
and two tiny legs kicked.
Now Bill and Edith were excited, as any new parents can be,
but what's an appropriate name, for the 'new branch' on their family tree?
"Suzie", was a bundle of energy, right from the start,
with a smile that would warm, the coldest of hearts.
Soon there was a thatch of blonde hair, and sparkling blue eyes,
of true finnish decent, no one could deny.

Bathed by the 'Keweenaw' sun, warm clean sand and blue lake,
helped develop his little girl, to the beautiful young lady,
one day she would make.

Now for the record, and her mom will agree,
she was not exactly the angel, they hoped she would be!!
Rowdy and feisty, she had a mind of her own,
but about the time of her teens, much finesse had been honed.

A sharp young lady, at the top of her class,
she loved music and sports, but too soon these years passed.
Now it was off to the city, for this university bound lass,
and four years of hard work, but a rank high in her class.

To be a 'dental hygienist', was formost on her mind,
and the type of person it takes, Sue sure was that kind.
She was conscientious, and gentle and related well with everyone,
charming smile, and sense of humor, she sure could be fun.
With her diploma in hand, she returned to the U.P.,
a very talented professional, and all her patients agree.

Somethings have not changed, from that wee Susan Faye,
she's still feisty, and independent, and humorous games she still plays,
she's still a blonde blue eyed beauty, but evolved from a young lass,
to a mature young women, with considerable class.

Sue, I know your moms proud, and me too my true friend,
so please remain close, 'till He chooses our end.

Teasin'

Yes you do, now don't deny,
and don't say that you don't really try,
as it's always there in the fetching smile,
and twinkling eyes, there's no denial.

Some tease in a way it really hurts,
but you're just a kidding sassy flirt,
and you do it in such an artful way,
like cat and mouse in a game of play.

You're teasin' now, I know you are,
that devious smile and eyes twinkling like a star,
and a laugh that fills you so with glee,
a happy teasin' lady is what I see.

Friend, you laugh and tease in such a way,
just like pure sunshine every day,
so go ahead and laugh at me,
just promise to keep teasin' 'till eternity.

Teddy Bear

Oh! teddy bear so very real, is what I see,
and how I feel, as you snuggle close,
and I hold you tight, how warm you feel,
throughout the night, and you don't complain,
when I'm fast asleep, so close to me you always keep.

Those large brown eyes that really care,
and big heart inside that wants to share.
Your touch so warm, the feelings great,
and you are so neat, and it really shows,
'cause you soothe my heart, as together we grow.

Of all the bears that do abound,
there's not another like you around.
I hope and pray that you're not just a dream,
and with your promise to be always there,
you snugly special teddy bear.

Your hidden dimple and smile so neat,
is our secret that we both will keep,
'cause no one else will take the time,
to share some love and really care,
to fully appreciate you, my teddy bear.

The November Wind

That whistling wind blows from the North,
and holds bent the leafless trees.
What now is a biting winter wind,
a short time ago was a summer breeze.

Tall frozen maple trees seem entombed,
their creaks and groans sound a haunting refrain.
They'll have to endure several months of this,
before the wind brings the warm spring rains.

To you, like me, who have heard the sounds,
it means a change in the season, we know.
While that cold north wind teases tree tops,
their roots are at rest under a blanket of snow.

Go ahead November wind pour it on,
with all your savage might,
as my cozy log cabin will keep you out,
and my fireside is especially comfy tonight.

The Truth

Truth is golden, a most precious trait,
use it always, when you relate.
It builds strong friendships, with those that you meet,
as trust is something, that everyone seeks.

How great it is, when you can believe,
what friends tell you, and their not out to deceive.

Kindness

An act of kindness, do you know what it means?
When last did you use it, search your memory to see.
The portion of kindness, of which you may share,
Is a determining factor, but also just that you care.

How fulfilling for those, who make an effort each day,
to distribute some kindness, when at work and at play.

Thanksgiving

The first years for the Pilgrims,
were so very rough indeed,
as they cleared out the forest to plant the tiny seeds.
The Indians they befriended,
gave them pumpkin, squash, and corn or maze,
and the sharing was appreciated in many many ways.

These first bountiful harvest,
must of been exciting to behold,
and were stored away for winter, before the days grew cold.
The Pilgrims were so very thankful,
and knelt daily in their prayers,
but they wanted to show the Indians, just how much they cared.

On one late November day,
Pilgrims and Indians gathered one and all,
to share the bountiful harvest, and game from the forest tall.
From that humble feast of joy,
became the real beginning,
of an annual family dinner, we all now call Thanksgiving.

To give thanks this time of year,
fulfills so many hearts, but also daily thanks,
through love and prayers, where God has played His part.
My life's been blessed so very much,
through all my daily living,
so I respond to let him know, and not just on Thanksgiving.

Two Hearts

Deep secrets in ones heart can lay,
to bring forth fond memories,
of those days when we were oh so very close,
and often played at things we loved the most.

Both hearts entwined and burst with love,
encouraged on by Him above to share with us,
the joys we seek, as we reached out,
to touch, and memories keep.

Nostalgic dreams of days just past,
yes, deep inside where they do last, to come alive,
at each new dawn encouraging a special love to carry on,
and fulfill the dreams so newly spawned.

Listen my dear to what hearts say,
and not seek out our separate ways, for we,
yes us, have endured and loved,
and are so richly blessed by Him above.

Two Hearts Entwined

Two hearts entwined,
yet floating free,
on a golden chain,
for all to see.

Our Love so blessed,
by Him above,
we have a special life,
to live and love.

To Share

Do you ever consider the wealth you have,
and the satisfaction that comes when you share.
This is something you should really consider,
and don't say that you really don't care.

You don't have to donate monetary items,
but just let someone know that you care.
You're constantly acquiring knowledge and things,
and there's many who wished you would share.

You may love to cook, or tinker with cars,
and you feel that your carpenter work is just fair,
but please don't always work by yourself,
'cause you may learn from someone else, when you share.

To a shut-in at home, or in a hospital bed,
even a short visit shows that you care.
And if you're sincere and stop by and see them,
you'll feel great,'cause you took time to share.

It's the simple things that all of us have,
and it doesn't take a lavish affair,
to serve up things like love, a smile, or tenderness,
and often you get more in return when you share.

Touch Me

I can not explain, nor do I try,
the warmth I feel when you're close by,
or what starts me tingling deep inside,
when you touch my hand and eyes meet eyes.

Our lips are silent and oh it's great,
how lucky are we who communicate,
with a gentle touch or a little squeeze,
like raindrops caress petals on a soft summer breeze.

We all have this ability but unless we try,
we'll not communicate with a touch and the eyes.
You are very special to come through as you do,
these vibes whisper softly, "I really love you".

"The Saga of Slick Willie"

What happened to "Our White House", when entered by Pres. Hillary,
or that "waffle" guy she brought along, of course it was "Slick Willie."
We were just recovering from 'Agnew,' and a more familiar look,
who kept pointing a finger in the mirror, and said, "I'm not a crook."

We slowly turned the corner, as credibility did return,
and we were ready for it, and how very much we yearned.
Starting with the Fords, then Carter, and both Reagans,
then George, and special Barbara, yes it did return again.

But now the Nixon years looked maybe even mild,
as Hillary & Willie came on like that dreadful brackish tide.
She the past president, of the "Pack" known as trial lawyers,
and he the "Oxford" scholar, yes two educated Liars.

Our beautiful respected White House, and the time honored Oval Room,
now no one can be trusted, and how disgraceful the new name "Oral Room."
That lovely, and honest secretary, "Betty," who served so many Presidents,
it must be a constant nightmare with both of these new residents.

Willie's escapades, recorded by Jennifer Flowers,
who are you who voted for the one entrusted with such power?
Of course it would by "Monica," to disclose so many more,
like Paula Jones and Katherine Wiley, I'm glad we're not keeping score!!

I know we should be forgiving, but there's something we wish you'd tell,
why did you use "Our" White House, rather than a trailer or motel?
You denied us an answer, and preferred Sec. Betty would tell instead
how all your gifts to "Monica," turned up beneath her bed?

Slick Willie Sage
Page II

Also Slick Willie, about your V.P. and "inventor," Al Gore,
a liar also, but unfortunately has NO memory, to keep score!!!
Would you both advise us to tell the truth, and also do agree,
to be a better person under God,and not like Gore,drink too much iced tea?

Did George Washington appear before you one night, to assist your "Legacy,"
and said just tell the truth like, "Yes, I chopped down the cherry tree?"
Then the following night when Thomas Jefferson did appear,
and advised," just really slash the taxes, and your "Legacy" will be clear?"
But best advice, the following night, when Abe Lincoln came in sight,
and said, "to really have a "Legacy," go the the Washington theatre tonight!"

You know that Ford pardoned Nixon, but you can't do it to yourself,
we know you'll do it for Web Hubble, Jim and Susan McDougal, and whom-ever
else? In order to protect you and Hillary from your crime,
they pleaded the 5th., and went to prison for you, to do "their time.
We have often tried to tell you, that you "have" established "your" Legacy,
now in history it is recorded, for all the world to ever see.

We could talk more about Lincoln's bedroom, but it really makes us sick,
'cause now with all the "traffic," it's known as "Motel Six!"
It's time to "leave" Our White House," please take along Hillary and Al Gore,
then we can again have "Honesty," Creditability," and be so proud once more.

Humor VS Hurt

Humor, like beauty, is in the eye of the beholder,
and is enhanced, like getting wiser, as we turn a little older.
Humor comes in many forms so you must be in control,
to concentrate and shape it, to achieve a healthy goal.

Is your humor caustic and degrading, or happy and delightful,
depending on your present mood, let's hope that it is plausible?
As you share with others, on life's undulating trail,
your humor can be therapeutic, to the strong, and yes also to the frail.

Hurtful humor often offends some very different lifestyles,
like homosexuals, gays, and lesbians, as today we often profile.
Once called fags, queers, and fairies, we were not very discreet,
like when two "fairies" first saw an auto "ferry" and said, " I know
our group is large, but I never knew we had a fleet?"

It's kind of like ethnic profiling, which hurts a certain race,
so we must reach out to these poor souls, as we look into their face.
As this attitude that we have can easily be reversed,
as a smile comes more easily, and we'll not be forever cursed.

My Paula, a dark skin beauty, one of my most special friends,
has a radiant smile, and humor, I hope will never end.
I once said, "you dance so beautifully" and she said, "you are forgiven,"
with a lovely smile, and twinkling eyes, she said, "'cause we've got rhythm"!!!

When you mention 'ethnic profiling,'this immediately comes to mind,
so many dark skin people are a very special kind,
like my Paula, Michael Jordan, Harry Belafonte, and Martin Luther King,
and don't forget Mohammed Ali, Oprah Winfry, all names with a very special ring.

So use your humor wisely, and not the kind that really hurts,
like those shady 'ladies, who like to tease, tantalize and flirt!!!
And how about Red Skelton, Bob Hope, and many more,
who's humor made them millions, and also friends galore?

"Young Birthday Man"

The second year into your teens,
so your 14 years of age.
Do you know just what it means,
or is it just the turning of another page?

Ben we are really proud of you,
'cause you really have matured,
but many problems we went through,
when you were a difficult fledgling 'bird'!!!

The past six months you tried real hard,
to become someone responsible,
before that you were a real card,
and we thought maturing was impossible!

So have a real happy birthday,
and many more to come,
we love you very much each day,
and you're a "Special" beautiful son.

“Pets ‘n Kids”

I can’t imagine kids growing up without pets in their life,
it’s like salt without pepper, having pets and kids, and a caring wife.
They’re an intregal part of family and fun,
and the greeting of a “wagging” tail when your days work is done.

You must choose the right pets, to grow up with you,
to teach kids responsibility, caring, loving in all that they do.
It’s an important decision fitting pets with your child,
is it for a gentle girl, or a boy who can get a little wild!!!

That playful cuddly fuzzy kitty, or a “rowdy” young pup,
and kitties are all so cute when little, ‘cats’ eventually grow up.
Dogs need to be walked ‘daily’, and don’t forget the ‘bag’,
after ‘dumping’ on the neighbors grass a tail proudly wags!!!

If you’re not home much, should it be a dog, or a bird,
just remember the farmer stuck at home milking a 7 day dairy herd?
The miniature poodle can go, but the “St. Bernard” takes a whole car,
and consider the ‘potty’ stops if you’re traveling very far.

Most kids grow up more responsible, loving, and do care,
if their life includes pets, when ‘all’ things they must share.
We’ve raised five very special caring siblings,
who shared a “Zillion pets,” and ‘most times’ were willing!!!

There was Mickey & Snooker, a very special dog and cat,
and flying things like Blackie the crow, tropical birds, but ‘no’ not a bat.
There were Barney, Sparky, Bo,Cybil, and a squirrel called ‘Hairy’,
a white rat “wiskers,” some mice, gerbils, all tame, but a ‘pack that
was scary!

"Pets 'n Kids" Page II

They were the 5 six week old wolf pups, dug from a den,
by a 'bounty' hunter who for the money would turn them in.
A friend, and I, paid him the price to keep them alive,
but they howled and growled, and sometimes nasty, when months turned to five.

They were fuzzy and fun at first, in a nice cage in my basement,
but then came a time I thought was fun, but then to my amazement,
when my sister and husband came to town to visit for the weekend,
later told friends her bad brother bunked her in the basement with them!!!

Then two ferrets, especially a neat 'Sierra,' and a couple of fuzzy bunnies
several turtles, snakes, and "waterloo," the wood chuck, 'nasty' and not very funny.
Some neighbors thought we "dropped from a tree, "or just" went to the dogs,"
but we felt we were very "sane, 'cause we never ever had frogs!!!

Now as we reflect, in the twilight years of our life,
we just have purrrfect "Laser Kitty," and just very little strife.
We would do it all again as our kids are very special, and do agree,
you too should add some neat pets, to your 'family tree.'

Lucas and Fuzzy

"Ethnic Profiling"

Ethnic profiling may sound harsh to you,
but certainly not too me,
'cause it really depends on where you 'hang your hat,'
and for most of my life mine has been Michigan's U.P.

It's not just the blacks, or bronzed Latinos,
and many other minorities scattered around,
but the 'varied' whites and Native Americans,
in God's country the U.P., where we have many 'Ethnic' towns.

My long wonderful life in Upper Michigan,
has made me partial, yes indeed,
'cause I've honed my 'ethnic profiling',
and it's the Finn's, not like me a Swede.

I can now spot most Finn's, a few steps away,
but when they talk is all that I need,
as they continue to walk in their own happy way,
with a friendly, "piva-piva", like "enjoy this very day."

There's Toivo, and buddy Eino, who often makes us smile,
also Hilda, Signe and Impie, who are very special cooks
like yummy "Kahvi-leipa", and "kala moiaka" soup,
but Tauno and Sulo, more appreciate their very good looks!!!

Most Finn girls are <u>real</u> blondes, with friendly sky blue eyes,
and I've "profiled" more than a few myself,
and the fun times we shared together,
I considered my long remembered wealth.

My friends today seem so perplexed,
as I rattle off their special sounding names,
and at times like this I often do reflect,
on my many finnish friends, and all our fun and games.

There's Seppanens, Juntinens, and my friend Rudy Pennala,
Emil Witinen, the logger, and friend Wesley Wentela,
also Coy Hill, Ski Jumper, and the famous "Flying Bietilas,"
Nestor Norkoli, log cabin builder, and well driller Ed Hakala.

"Ethnic Profiling" Page II

Those special blondes to 'profile', like Suzy Isaacson,
Connie Maki, Betty Juntila, and I can't forget Edna Pynnonen.
Also my life long friends, Clyde Tuomela, and Herby Hytinen,
TV6 anchor Carl Pellonpaa, and "professor, " Marty Eskelinen!!!

When I built my cabin on beautiful clean Lake Superior,
it was fondly known as "Suomi Seashore,"
as there were neighbors like; Nevelas, Heikkilas, John Akkala,
an no doubt several more.

To hunt at "Sumpo Lodge," in a cedar swamp, you had to be a Finn,
owners included Sheriff Al Jacobson, and Sulo Victor Hytinen.
A strange song 'boomed' out many nights, after the beer and wine,
maybe the Finnish Anthem? "Peeki-siki.peeki-sika.porky pine!!!

Us 'want to be Finns' like friend, " Reino Lutey-Kinnen,"
called me "Weesa-maki" "are you a Finn he would tout"?
I would respond, to his wife's dismay, "if you are 'ethnic profiling,'
why certainly, I'm half Finn, and also half out"!!!

My list would never be complete without Wilho Tuominen,
a special 'top-notch' carpenter, who naturally is a Finn.
Wilho, my business building partner, could really drive a nail,
but I didn't share that "kala-moiaka" (fish head soup), in his dinner pail!!!

When I first met Ingrid Bartelli, "mushroom professor,"
she said, "Bud, I've heard that you are a 'legend in your own time,"
so I told my partner Wilho this, and he countered with,
" I'm sure she said, "you are a legend in you own 'mind' "!!!

Toivo looking for brother Eino in back of house smelled something 'Rank',
there was Eino, with a pole poking in his 'septic tank'.
Eino answering Toivo's question, "I'm looking for my jacket,
and I know it will be ruined, but there's a 'pasty' in the pocket"!!!

Well by now you know very well, that I would just be lying,
if I said, " I didn't enjoy my ethnic Finnish profiling."
Some day I'll tell the world, what now is just a rumor,
how lucky for us who experienced that 'classic' Finnish humor"!!!

'Teen Time'

Today son Lucas you're a teen,
the years have gone so fast,
it's almost like a special dream.
'cause you're now a young man with real class.

When you were just a little 'tyke',
I carried, and sang, many nights to you,
now you do 'wheelies' on your bike,
and you're my 'special' helper buddy too.

No better partner could I find,
when we traveled to Florida and Cal. State,
and our Alaska trip went super fine,
and Washington, D.C. trip, a memorable special date.

Now you're so very tall and strong,
and it seems we did 'most' things right,
when very few things went wrong,
and daily 'adjustments' oh so slight.

So good in school, and also sports,
I hope you'll stay on track,
obey the laws, and out of courts,
and you will avoid much nasty flak.

You're the most precious one in the whole wide world,
to me, and your mother too,
so please 'listen' to us and you'll know why,
we want to share so much with you.

"Legal Beagles"

**I'm a hunter, and 'all' hunting has a limited season,
but for 'Legal Beagles' there's an 'Open Season', for valid reason.
Mostly because of their century old dishonesty, and lack of respect,
I will document 'proof', so you can digest their acts, then reflect.**

**Only 'tactful' way to describe a 'L.B.', in their own "Jargon and diatribe," is this
quiz, according to 'L.B.', 'Slick Willie', "What is the real 'meaning', of the
word " is "!! Also, I never shake hands with a Legal Beagle',
'cause you'll get a bill for, "Services rendered," (25.00) is that really legal?**

**Respected Paul Harvey, 15 yrs. ago, reported a riot in Kremlin Red Square,
of students turning cars over, and burning, but no 'proof', as he wasn't there?
Caught 'Red handed' (no pun!)' with many witnesses, large and small,
with-in an hour they were given a 'fair trial' - <u>guilty</u>', and shot against a wall!!!**

**Paul said he doesn't completely agree with system, but it may be fair,
as they have so very few riots, in Russia's Kremlin Red Square!!
He also said, "We have 42' L.B.' per 10,000 people in U.S., while only '2' in Japan,
that's why we have so many more problems, and create the Tax payers 'SCAM'?**

**We saw an example of two 'L.B.' in 'Pres.' Hillary, and Willy's, years '92 to 01',
with 'White water', Monica, and all these 'lies' will 'haunt' them in years to come.
I may be a bit impartial, but owning a ski area business,
where 'L.B.', and all the "nusience claims", just doesn't make legal sense.**

**Also ironic humor when they say, " no fee 1st visit, just bring in financial
statement,as assets will determine how many 'L.B.', and length of case,
and of course 'E-Z' payments!!! If you had 7-8 million it will take a whole team,
for over a year, and even if you brutally murdered your spouse and friend
they'll save your rear!!!**

**Up North we can tell if it's really cold, when bike chain slips on the sprocket,
or if we see a 'L.B.' with hands in 'their <u>own</u> pockets.
When Slick Willie denied he 'groped that nice aide, saying it was silly,
'cause he just likes 'endowed' girls like Monica, not small type like
Catherine Willy!!**

"Legal Beagles" Page II

**When U.S. Bar Association passed resolution to make 'death penalty illegal,
because of their 'humanitarianism', compassionate' feelings, of the Legal beagles?
Why cut off 'cash flow' from repeat' offenders, which we all agree,
would be like removing all the 'Pork barrels,' in Washington, D.C.?**

**Clark Gifford, wealthy 'L.B.' and advisor to six presidents, and true bureaucrat,
but what he did to BCC (Bank of Credit and Commerce), just a disgusting rat.
Convicted of 'lawndering' drug money, and bankrupting the bank,
now called BCC (Bank of Crooks and Convicts), and poor stock holders have
him to 'thank'.**

**With his team of crooked 'L.B.', paid for by his 'criminal' wealth,
at 82 yrs., they convinced court, he would die in prison because of poor health?
That was some years ago, and he's still 'outside' and alive,
"when you do the crime you do the time," so take it out of his 'hide'.**

**Willie in '92 and '96 'promised' swift justice to drug king pins, and peddlers,
with death penalty as answer, but there's been none, and system no better.!!
Remember Manuel Norriega, Panama drug king, 15 yrs. now in Florida 'prison',
supported by 'Tax payers 'L.B., and no one understands the reason?**

**Did anyone forget 5 yrs. ago when McVey bombed Oklahoma Federal Building,
Murdered 160, including 30 children, some federal workers siblings?
Next day 'L.B. 'Slick Willie, on TV, promised us all,
'swift' action, and with in <u>one year</u>, responsible ones, 'shot at the wall'?
Tim McVey convicted <u>5 years</u> ago, with 'L.B. keeping him in a cell,
he keeps pleading for death, but not while 'tax payers' L.B. doing so well?**

**Some years ago a 'L.B.' wealthy senator, married, but at party with 'friend'
it ended in 'wee' hours, and unfortunately brought her 'young' life to an end.
He was driving her 'home' when he drove off bridge in car with them in it,
he was a strong college swimmer when car sunk, in the river Chappiquiticc.**

**He swam to the surface, but it ended up being her 'tomb',
'cause he didn't take her up with him for some 'breathing room'?
He had a good 'L.B.', "fair" Justice hearing, and 'he' survived,
he got off 'scott' free, but she's no longer alive.**

**I often think of 'Maude' from her series on T.V.,
saying, "God will get you for it", while pointing finger for us all to see.
'L.B.' just laugh, and continue, like life's just a 'piece of cake,
it's disgusting, and we don't like it, so <u>please</u> - "give us a break"**

"Legal Beagles" Page III

When we all die, most of us Christians agree,
the path after death has one fork we will see.
One is shining bright and going up North to the Heaven,
the other fork South goes down to a very hot oven?

In '92 when Clintons and George Bush, were going to Inaugural for first time,
their 'Limo" totally crashed, while driving in line.
arriving at 'Pearly gate', St. Peter sitting in chair, to decide their fate,
when asked, Willie said, "I was incoming president, but will be a bit late!!

St. Pete said, " sit to my right, as a good resource person you will be,
he had Bush sit in left chair, saying, " you too can help I agree.
Then looking at Hillary he said, " and you are - lady so fair"?
her typical 'firm' answer, " I'm Hillary and your in '<u>my</u>' chair!!

Some others like Spiro Agnew, Nixon, Sen. Packwood, and other familiar names,
like Dan 'Rotten Kowski', Web Hubble, McDougals, all in "crooks hall of fame"!!
finally Marc Rich, 'L.B.' Jack Quinn, with 'illegal' millions for defense,
unfortunately 'tax payers' it's so ridiculous, and certainly makes no sense?

Maybe we should have special penalty for 'Legal Beagles', 'On the hill,'
like they do for other dogs like 'Pitbulls' that kill?
We should leash and 'muzzle' them, but cause them no pain,
and give them 'Life term' in animal shelter, or is that too 'humane'?

So fellow tax payers 'stay' alert, and trust in your luck,
as the 'Beagles' will fleece us, and take all of our hard earned bucks?
Need I wonder if the 'L.B.' Bar Association "Beueaurcrats",
will ask me to be their special "Poet Laureate"?

Twilight - Trails End

**In the year of '27, a new life born with help from Heaven,
a feisty baby boy, who's parents thought a real joy,
but wait, we're they prepared for this, as only time would tell,
was it really 'a bundle of joy', or constant work with a diaper smell!!**

**This first boy, a proud Mom and Dad, emerged crying and so little,
at 'home', in small logging town, some 30 miles from only hospital.
It was Big Bay, Michigan, with Dad at work in the lumber mill,
and when told of sons birth, he trotted home, just 2 blocks up the hill.**

**With the Lord always by my side, throughout the ensuing years,
there were lots of highs, and at times those normal tears.
The family grew with 2 more boys and sisters, for a total of five,
and when I became a father, I had the same, and they filled me with pride.**

**In this forest land, with clean cold lakes, an 'outdoor' man soon took shape,
my Mom too fished, and hunted with me, and taught me to cook and also bake.
I was fair in school, but most important were my many friends,
and remain close today, with great memories, at twilight, and the trails end.**

**Very active in all sports, throughout Junior and Senior high school,
and although 'scrappy', and stood my ground, but did obey the 'Golden Rule'!
World War II, did change my life, as all the young men left town,
I joined the U.S. Navy at age 17, to 'explore' the world around.**

**For over a year I "toured" the South Pacific, with many exotic names,
Guam and Eniwetok Islands, Ulithi in Carolinas, and the Marshal Island,
Kwajalein.
Also Phillipines and Hawaii too, where I met the only "hula-hula" girl,
mother later in humor said, is she the one who caused your hair to 'curl'?**

**Back home again I started college, as was expected of you to do,
pursuing a Forestry Degree, and got my private pilots license too.
Then with friend Bernie, and only $200 cash between us, we hitched hike West,
with goal being Alaska, but funds ran out, so logging was our next test!!**

**We got a job in Cascade Mtns., close by Sweet Home, Oregon,
had to 'charge' our new 'cork boots' (spiked), as law said you must put them on.
Super camp food, and exciting time, and they kept your butt in gear,
much sweat all day, then 'quick' dip in cold Calipooey Creek, frosted up your
rear!!!**

Twilight - Trails End Page II

Then back home to get 'real' life started, on 'multiple' careers,
in auto business, building contractor, ski area owner, and fun nights with foaming
beers. The highlight thru this all included a special classy gal,
she liked outdoor sports, a sharp R.N., but best of all a real pal.

She was a Super Mother to our kids, and many pets alike,
and did her share in all our projects, and enjoyed trails that we hiked.
Like building two new homes ourself, and especially the big country one,
160 'prime' acres, creek with trout pond, 4000 sq. ft. tri-level, open to the sun.

Two large fireplaces, cedar paneled sauna, with a long deck on three sides,
large living room, with 45' of curved glass wall, brought nature right inside.
Early in our marriage, with help from the kids, we also built a cabin,
on beautiful Lake Superior, and I still consider it a 'special' piece of Heaven.

We recorded this on 5 movie films, as it started from standing trees,
cut by me, on 'snowshoes', with my chain saw, and put together in 'degrees'.
Cut logs, then skid by horse to logging truck, to sawmill, sawed then 'sticker-
piled', lumber hauled to site, and weekend built, when weather soon turned mild.

Our natural 'knotty-pine' paneling, open beams, and central stone fireplace,
has kitchen side B-B-Q, to grill our favorite, "flambeau onion sirloin steak".
Each evening the fireplace 'dancing flames', casts shadows on one wall,
with large bull moose trophy, 2 nice bucks, and other 'critters', large and small.

The large picture window has a beautiful, ever changing scene,
of Lake Superiors' crashing waves, and roaring, as we drift into our dreams.
The Worlds best therapy, with warm sunny days, and clear starry nights,
and the four changing seasons, create delightful nature sights.

Another of the 'highlights' is my 15 years as a 'Ski-doo' retailer,
and many weekends when I raced, and hauled several on our trailer.
I was lucky to have a super mechanic Dave, who tuned them to perfection,
and I often finished right on top, and our sleds always passed 'inspection'.
I finished 3rd one year in World series, at Eagle River. Wis. race,
and in North American Championship, and over 300 sleds, I finished
in 2nd Place.

Over 18 years in Rotary Club, a past president, and we served our city well,
a great 'Anti-litter' project, helped handicapped kids, and 7 yrs. I rang Sal. Army
Christmas Bell. Also many years a Vice Chairman, with National Ski Hall of
Fame, raised new building funds, and inducted olympic Medal winners,
with familiar names.

Twilight - Trails End Page III

I owned a ski area for 12 years, much fun, but also some difficult times,
just a small percentage of customers creating problems, and crimes.
Too much pressure by 'Legal-beagles', with bar, and many college students at night, food service, ski lift inspectors, OSHA, 'nuisance claims', and always 'others' rights!!!

Lots of benefits like fun loving people, and my family use of place,
enjoying skiing, 'frisbee' tourneys, wedding receptions, and watching skiers race.
Also I could enjoy U.S. ski areas, without always being 'on call',
like skiing East, and especially West, where the mountains are so tall.

The Lord is with me 'daily', and 'together' we've done so many things,
I enjoyed my time in the church choir, and still enjoy Sunday songs we sing.
He's enriched my families life, with excellent health, and all we've shared,
I thank Him often 'daily', and there's 'ample' evidence He really cares.'

I'm often asked what I did in life, and my answer is always the same,
in 4 business ventures, but my retirement most successful, so there I will remain!!!
After 45 years of poetry, mostly for friends, and for myself,
nice to have several published Nationally, but it hasn't helped my wealth!!
The honor I got from the ISP (International Society of Poets), in Washington, D.C., and 'peer pressure' to print my book, is an incentive to continue, and exciting for me.

With much help from Him above, plus daily work out, and healthy diet,
should give me a few more years, before I'm eternally "quiet"!!
I have a 'resting place' for my ashes, a large stone with verse I've penned,
" I did it my way with much help from the Lord - Amen."

Index Page

Icons

Humor · Special People · † Spiritual Faith · Special Places · ●Nationaly published poems

Pearls to ponder:

My Philosophy:

A. I never have a bad day - but some are better than others!
B. Don't take life too seriously, as you never get out alive!
C. Don't sweat the little things - and every thing is little!

1. Ones life can be like a stagnant pool, unless the surface is sprinkled daily with humor.
2. Shed your cocoon of discontent, take flight, the beautiful world awaits you.
3. How lucky you really are is quite evident, you're alive - enjoy.
4. Yes, I'll enjoy today 'cause I'm able to, and I'm not sure about tomorrow.
5. Dusk fades into darkness, exciting tomorrow is just a dream away.
6. How fortunate are we who can recognize the deep inner beauty in others.
7. How fortunate are the really beautiful people who's natural warmth and inner beauty builds strong and lasting friends.
8. Everyone is implanted with the seed of natural and sincere understanding, and if nurtured, will reap a harvest of true and lasting friendships.
9. Envy is real, recognize this, but culture ones own beautiful attributes and you too will find it's gratifyingly contagious.
10. Why dwell on the attributes you feel others possess, but utilize this time to develop ones own latent talents,and reap the beautiful rewards of your endeavors.
11. Recognize the beautiful things one surrounds themselves with, and you to will reflect these redeeming qualities.
12. The idle promise to oneself to slow the hectic pace is a pathetic gesture, but worse yet if one believes it, without at least a vain effort to pursue.
13. Unbelievingly beautiful becomes ones world when they assimilate, and share, those every day joys that abound in ones environment.

Pearls to ponder: Page II

14. How productive and gratifying to utilize the time one wastes from complaning by recognizing, and developing ones latent attributes, which we harbor in limitless quantities.

15. Beauty is definitely is in the eye of the beholder, but how unfortunate that the beholder so often can not recognize the beauty laying dormant within themselves.

16. Relay the beautiful true feelings that you recognize in someone else and the bond and rapport that results will magnify and grow with each successive meeting.

17. Only genuine, and honest, compliments will endour in time as false, and insincere, words will dissipate immediately creating a deeper void than may have currently existed.

18. Even a 'grouch' does not want to do business with a 'grouch'!

19. A warm fuzzy kitty, with audible purr, produces a very therapeutic, and soothing, 'placebo', but may cause an addiction!!

20. Putting ones brain in gear 'before' opening mouth, enhances a more positive communication.

21. Using smiles, and hugs, daily can become addictive, and build more positive, and exciting, relationships.

22. Sharp, but friendly wit, outlasts, and enhances relationships, while a 'sharp' tongue creates diametrical results.

23. If you display less noticeable optimism about your success', than your peers do about you, you may possess some humility.

24. Signs on city sanitation truck?
    A. You must be satisfied. or double your garbage back!!
    B. Equal opportunity employer: minimum wage and all you can eat!!

25. 'Ex-lady friend'; double weight problem 'full figure' and 'heavy' drinker!!
    'Current lady friend'; 'healthy' weight, attractive, blue eyed blonde, with neat humor!!

26. We get too quick old, and too late smart.